DOGS

COCKER SPANIELS

STUART A. KALLEN

ABDO & Daughters

Published by Abdo & Daughters, 4940 Viking Drive, Suite 622, Edina, Minnesota 55435.

Library bound edition distributed by Rockbottom Books, Pentagon Tower, P.O. Box 36036, Minneapolis, Minnesota 55435.

Printed in the United States.

Cover Photo credit: Peter Arnold, Inc.

Interior Photo credits: Peter Arnold, Inc.

Edited by Rosemary Wallner

Library of Congress Cataloging-in-Publication Data

Kallen, Stuart A., 1955
Cocker Spaniel / Stuart A. Kallen.
    p.   cm. — (Dogs)
Includes bibliographical references (p.24) and index.
   ISBN 1-56239-452-5
1. Cocker spaniels—Juvenile literature. [1. Cocker spaniels. 2. Dogs.] I. Title. II. Series
Kallen, Stuart A., 1955- Dogs.
SF429.C55K35 1995
636.7'52—dc20   95-2238
                                                  CIP
                                                  AC

ABOUT THE AUTHOR
Stuart Kallen has written over 80 children's books, including many environmental science books.

Contents

DOGS AND WOLVES: CLOSE COUSINS

Dogs have been living with humans for more than 12,000 years. Today, hundreds of millions of dogs live in the world. Over 400 **breeds** exist.

All dogs are related to the wolf. Some dogs—like tiny poodles or Great Danes—may look nothing like the wolf. But under their skin, all dogs share the same **instincts** and **traits** as the wolf.

The dog family is called Canidae, from the Latin word meaning "dog." The canid family has 37 **species**, including foxes, jackals, wild dogs, and wolves.

All dogs are related to the wolf. This is a gray wolf in a northern Montana forest.

COCKER SPANIELS

Cocker spaniels are playful and lovable. Although no one knows for sure, spaniels probably came from Spain. That's why they were given the name "spaniels." Spaniels come from a long line of hunters. They were among the first dogs ever trained as hunters.

Before the invention of rifles and shotguns, hunters used dogs and trained **birds of prey** to capture small **game birds**. First, a trained falcon or hawk was set free to circle in the sky. This would scare the game birds into hiding. Then the spaniel would flush the birds from their hiding places. The hunters captured the birds by throwing a net over the birds and the dog.

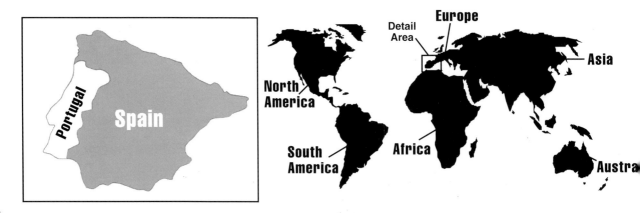

Spaniels are known for their jumping or "springing" skill.

Some larger spaniels jumped or "sprang" on their **prey**. They became known as "springer" spaniels. Smaller spaniels could crawl through dense **brush**. They were very good at hunting a bird called a woodcock. Those spaniels were called "cocker" spaniels.

WHAT THEY'RE LIKE

Cocker spaniels make lovable pets. They are alert and cheerful. They will gladly sit on your lap.

Cocker's have a good sense of hearing. They can hear sounds that are too high-pitched for humans to hear. They can also pick up sounds that are four times farther away. But a floppy-eared dog like a cocker cannot hear as well as dogs that have erect, pointed ears.

Cockers have a keen sense of smell. They learn about their world by sniffing everything around them.

Because of their sense of smell, people have trained cockers to find lost children. Cockers find a missing person by sniffing something the child wore. Then they sniff around trying to match the same smell. Cockers have also saved lives by alerting people to the smell of gas or smoke.

Cocker spaniels make lovable pets. They are alert and cheerful.

COAT AND COLOR

Cocker spaniels have long, soft, silky **coats**. Some cockers have a flat coat, but most have wavy hair. Long hair grows on the ears, chest, underbody, and legs. This long hair gives the cocker a feathered look. Some cockers look as though they are wearing long, fringed skirts on each leg.

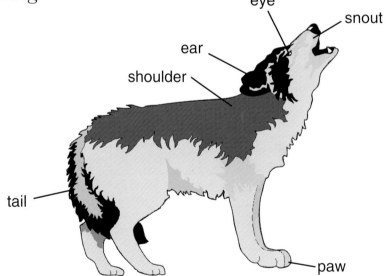

All dogs share the same features with their common ancestor, the wolf.

Cocker spaniels have long, soft, silky coats. This long hair gives the cocker a feathered look.

Cockers come in many different solid colors. The most common colors are golden brown, reddish brown, black, white, dark tan, or tan. Some cockers have coats that are two different colors. This is called parti-colored.

SIZE

The adult cocker spaniel measures about 15 inches (38 cm) from the ground to its shoulders. It weighs 23 to 28 pounds (10 to 12 kg). Its compact body has a broad chest supported by straight, powerful legs. Like any good hunting **breed**, cockers can keep up a fast pace for hours.

The cocker spaniel's head is well rounded with a square bold **muzzle**. The cocker has big eyebrows that give its face a sweet and funny expression. Cockers have slightly almond-shaped, dark brown eyes.

Cockers have long, floppy ears set low on the head. Some cockers have such long ears that they fall into the dog's food dish.

A **purebred** cocker spaniel is a beautiful dog. Few people can resist its friendly manner. Many people forget that the cocker was bred to be a great all-around hunting dog.

Because of its compact body and powerful legs, a cocker can run fast for many hours.

CARE

Cockers fit in well with most families. They are gentle, loving, playful and carefree. Although **bred** for hunting, cockers are not aggressive. This makes them good with children. Though cockers like to run free in the country, they also enjoy city living.

Like all dogs, cockers need the same things that humans need: a warm bed, food, water, exercise, and lots of love.

Cocker spaniels have long hair that needs daily brushing. If the dog is not **groomed**, its beautiful **coat** will become matted and tangled. Sometimes, the dog will need a bath and its nails clipped.

As a member of your household, your dog expects love and attention. Cockers enjoy human contact and like to **retrieve** sticks or catch Frisbees.

All dogs need shots every year. These shots help stop diseases such as **distemper** and **hepatitis**.

Cockers enjoy human contact and like to retrieve sticks or catch Frisbees.

FEEDING

Like all dogs, cocker spaniels enjoy meat. But cockers need a well-balanced diet. Most dog foods—dry or canned—will give the dog proper **nutrition**.

When you buy a puppy, find out what it has been eating and continue that diet. A small puppy needs four to five small meals a day. By six months, it will need only two meals a day. By one year, a single evening feeding will be enough.

Cockers must be exercised every day so they don't gain weight. Walking, running, and playing together will keep you and your dog happy and healthy. Give your dog a hard rubber ball with which to play.

Like any animal, cockers need a lot of fresh water. Water should be kept next to their food bowl and changed daily.

To grow up healthy and happy, cockers need a well-balanced diet.

THINGS THEY NEED

Dogs need a quiet place to sleep. A soft dog bed in a quiet corner is the best place for a cocker spaniel to sleep.

Cocker spaniels should live indoors. If the dog must live outside, give it a dry, **insulated** dog house.

Cockers love to run. A fenced-in yard is the perfect home for the dog. If that is not possible, use a chain on a runner.

In most cities and towns, dogs must be leashed when going for a walk. Dogs also need a license. A dog license has the owner's name, address, and telephone number on it. If the dog runs away, the owners can be called.

Cocker spaniels need baths to keep their coats lush and shiny.

PUPPIES

Average cocker spaniels can have three to five puppies. The dog is **pregnant** for about nine weeks. When she is ready to give birth, she needs a dark place away from noises. If your dog is pregnant, give her a strong box lined with an old blanket. She will have her puppies there.

Puppies are tiny and helpless when born. They arrive about half-an-hour apart. The mother licks them clean which helps them start breathing. Their eyes are shut, making them blind for their first nine days. They are also deaf for about ten days.

Dogs are **mammals**. They drink milk from their mother. After four weeks, puppies will grow teeth. Separate them from their mother and give the puppies soft dog food.

After being pregnant for nine weeks, a cocker spaniel will have three to five puppies.

GLOSSARY

BIRD OF PREY - A bird that eats meat.

BREED - A group of animals with the same traits; also to produce young.

BRUSH - Shrubs, bushes, and small trees growing thickly in the woods.

COAT - The dog's outer covering (hair).

DISTEMPER (dis-TEMP-pur) - A disease of dogs and certain other animals, caused by a virus.

GAME BIRD - A bird hunted for sport.

GROOM - To brush and take care of an animal.

HEPATITIS (hep-uh-TIE-tis) - The swelling of the liver caused by a virus.

INSTINCT - A way of acting that is born in an animal, not learned.

INSULATION (in-sue-LAY-shun) - Something that stops heat loss.

MAMMAL - A class of animals, including humans, that have hair and feed their young milk.

MUZZLE - The jaws, mouth, and nose of an animal.

NUTRITION (new-TRISH-un) - Food; nourishment.

PREGNANT - With one or more babies growing inside the body.

PREY - An animal hunted for food.

PUREBRED - Bred from members of one breed within a species.

RETRIEVE - To return or bring back.

SPECIES (SPEE-seas) - A plant or animal belonging to a particular classification.

TRAIT - A feature or characteristic.

Index

BIBLIOGRAPHY

American Kennel Club. *The Complete Dog Book*. New York: Macmillan, 1992.

Clutton-Brock, Juliet. *Dog*. New York: Alfred A. Knopf, 1991.

The Complete Book of the Dog. New York: Holt, Rinehart, & Winston, 1985.

Green, Carl R., and Sanford, William R. *The Cocker Spaniel*. New York: Crestwood House, 1990.

Nicholas, Anna Katherine. *A Complete Introduction to Cocker Spaniels*. Neptune City, N.J.: T. F. H. Publications, 1987.

Sylvester, Patricia. *The Reader's Digest Illustrated Book of Dogs*. New York: The Reader's Digest Association, 1984.